# Early I with JESUS

# God's Family

## The Ross family

Mum · Dad · Gran Ross · Grandpa Ross · Matthew · Nan Drew · Shags · Ben · Kate · Sparks

Published and produced by CWR, Waverley Abbey House, Waverley Lane, Farnham, Surrey GU9 8EP
Writer: Jenny King; Drawings: Harold King   Typeset by Watermark, Honing, Norfolk   Printed by Crusade Printing, Hampshire
ISBN 1—85345—056—1
©CWR 1992   All rights reserved. No part of this publication may be reproduced without the prior permission in writing of CWR
All Scripture quotations are from the Good News Bible   Copyright © American Bible Society, New York 1976

## NATIONAL DISTRIBUTORS

**AUSTRALIA:** Christian Marketing Pty Ltd., PO Box 154, N. Geelong, Victoria 3215. Tel: (052) 786100.
**CANADA:** Christian Marketing Canada Ltd., PO Box 7000, Niagara on the Lake, Ontario LOS 1JO. Tel: 416 641 0631.
**EIRE:** Scripture Union Book & Music Centre, 40 Talbot Street, Dublin 1. Tel: 363764.
**MALAYSIA:** Salvation Book Centre, (M) Sdn.Bhd, 23 Jalan SS2/64, 47300 Petaling Jaya, Selangor.
**NEW ZEALAND:** CWR (NZ), PO Box 4108, Mount Maunganui 3030. Tel: (075) 757412.
**NIGERIA:** F.B.F.M., No. 2 Mbu Close, S/W Ikoyi, Lagos.
**SINGAPORE:** Alby Commercial Enterprises·Pte Ltd., Garden Hotel, 14 Balmoral Road, Singapore 1025.
**SOUTHERN AFRICA:** CWR (Southern Africa), PO Box 43, Kenilworth 7745, RSA. Tel: (021) 7612560

# How to use Early Days

*Early Days* has been designed to help parents to teach simple Bible truths in an exciting and practical way.

Choose a quiet area to work and have the materials (if any) needed for the activity at hand. You will find it most helpful to use the Good News Bible as this is the version that the *Early Days* notes are based upon.

Read the Bible verse and then the story, and try to involve your child as much as possible. Encourage him/her to talk about the reading and the story and add your own comments. Try to help your child understand the theme.

Take time to do the activity for the day, but don't worry if you can't finish it or if you miss a few days. It's better to "get together" every other day for a longer time than to rush every day.

After you have completed the activity, say the prayer at the bottom of the page. Encourage your child to add to this prayer time, perhaps including people or situations that you think are relevant.

## *Harold and Jenny King*

 = Bible reading   = Prayer

 Psalm 105:4

Ben and Kate got up slowly. It was Sunday and there was plenty of time. But suddenly it was time to go! Ben couldn't find his shoe, Kate needed to have her hair brushed and Matthew still had breakfast all over his face!

Find Ben's shoe in this picture. .

 Dear Jesus, please help me to hurry when time is short.

 Proverbs 11:25

**At last they were ready. While Mum put Matthew in the car, Ben went to knock next door for Mrs Lloyd. During the week Mum took Mrs Lloyd shopping, and on Sundays they always gave her a lift to church.**

Colour in and cut out door (see last page). Hinge and stick.

 Dear Jesus, please show me ways I can help other people.

Ephesians 1:4-5

**Dad had gone off early to help get the church ready. There were chairs and hymn books to put out, the screen to put up and the communion table and lectern to get ready.**

Colour in and cut out furniture (see last page). Stick to picture.

Thank You, God, for people who help in church.

📖 Psalm 47:1-2

The family found four seats at the end of a row, with room for Matthew's pushchair next to them. The music group led two choruses, then after a prayer the pastor told the children the story of Samuel in the Temple.

Draw dot to dot (follow arrows).

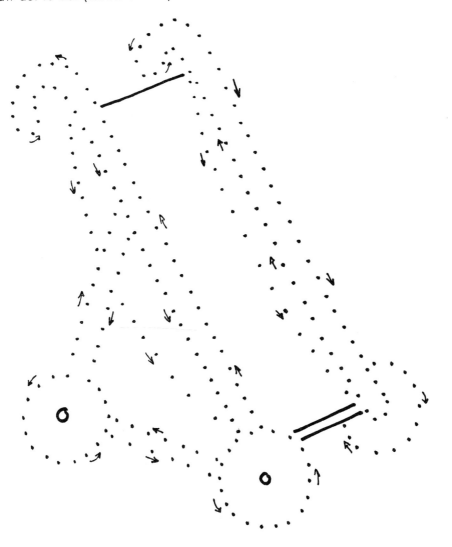

 Lord Jesus, I'm glad that we can sing to You.

 1 Samuel 1:11, 19–20

Hannah prayed to God: "Don't forget me! If you give me a son, I promise that I will dedicate him to you for his whole life." The Lord answered Hannah's prayer. She gave birth to a son. She named him Samuel and explained, "I asked the Lord for him."

Colour in

 Thank You, God, that You answer our prayers.

📖 1 Samuel 1:24–28

When Samuel was old enough to eat food, Hannah took him to Eli the priest at Shiloh. Hannah said to Eli, "Do you remember me? I am the woman you saw standing here, praying to the Lord. I asked Him for this child, and He gave me what I asked for. So I am dedicating him to the Lord. As long as he lives, he will belong to the Lord."

Colour in

 Dear Jesus, help me to keep my promises.

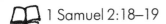 1 Samuel 2:18–19

As Samuel grew up he served the Lord in the Temple. Each year his mother would make a robe and take it to him, when she went with her husband to offer **the yearly sacrifice.**

Colour in

 Thank You, God, for my Mum.

📖 1 Samuel 3:2–10

One night Samuel heard a voice. It was God calling him. Samuel had never heard God before so he thought it was Eli the priest. God called two more times. Each time Samuel went to Eli. The third time Eli said, "It must be God calling; next time, Samuel, say, 'Speak Lord, Your servant is listening.'" The next time God spoke, Samuel said the words and God answered.

Colour in

Dear God, thank You for speaking to us through the Bible.

 Proverbs 23:12

After the children's talk Ben and Kate went out into Sunday School. Mum took Matthew into the creche.

Draw a picture of your Sunday School teacher.

Thank You, God, for our Sunday School teachers.

📖 Romans 5:8

This Sunday it was also communion. It was Dad's turn to pass around the bread and the little glasses of grape juice. The communion reminds Christians of Jesus' last supper and that Jesus died for us.

On a large sheet of paper make a collage of a loaf of bread using coloured paper and scraps torn from magazines etc.

 Dear Jesus, thank You for dying for me.

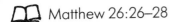 Matthew 26:26–28

Jesus was having supper with the disciples. He broke a piece of bread, said a prayer of thanks and gave it to them. He also gave them a cup of wine to share. The bread was to remind them of His body and the drink of His blood, because He would soon die so that our sins could be forgiven.

Colour in

 Dear Jesus, help me not to forget that You died for me.

 Psalm 27:1

After the service and Sunday School, Mum and Dad chatted to friends over coffee while the children played outside. When it was time to leave, Kate was nowhere to be found. But after a big search Dad found her helping Mrs Lloyd to wash up in the kitchen.

Which line will find Kate?

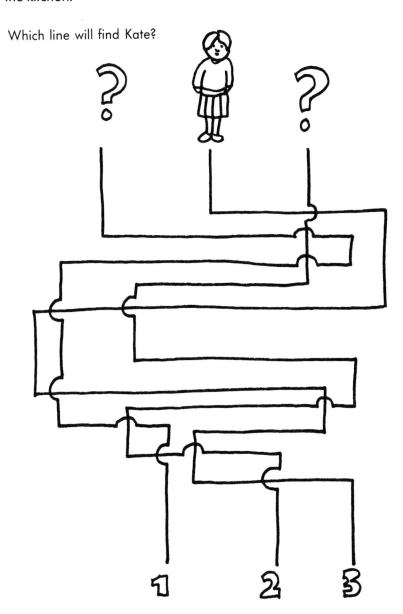

 Dear Jesus, please keep me from getting lost.

 Luke 2:41–45

When Jesus was 12 He went with His parents to the festival in Jerusalem. When the festival was over, Jesus stayed, but His parents didn't know this. They thought He was going back home with family or friends. They got worried when they couldn't find Him, so they went back to Jerusalem to look for Him.

Colour in

 Father God, help me to remember not to go off on my own without Mum or Dad.

📖 Luke 2:46–51

Jesus' parents found Him in the Temple after a long search. They were astonished to find Him talking with the Jewish teachers. They asked Him why he had stayed behind. Jesus told them He thought they would know He would be in His Father's house, but they didn't understand. He went back home with His parents and obeyed them.

Colour in

 Dear Jesus, help me to be obedient.

 Acts 2:46

Once home from church, Mum soon had the lunch on the table. Mrs Lloyd was eating with them and so was Mike. Mike was a student who had just started at the local college.

Draw your favourite lunch.

Thank You, God, for meals together.

 Psalm 25:16

It was Mike's first time away from home and he missed his local church. His church was very small and met in the local community centre. There was no one to play the piano, but one of the leaders sang with a guitar.

Two of each of the instruments are the same. Colour in the two that are the same.

 Dear Jesus, please be with people away from home.

 Psalm 24:1

As soon as lunch was over, the table cleared and the washing up done, Dad took Matthew upstairs for his sleep. Mum and Mrs Lloyd sat down for a chat, and then Dad and Mike took the children down to the park.

Find six differences in the pictures.

 Thank You, God, for outings.

 Romans 5:10-11

At the park Ben saw Guy, a new boy from his class at school. They played on the swings and slide while the Dads and Mike chatted. When it was time to go home, Ben asked if Guy could come to Boys' Brigade with him the next evening.

Cut slot to slide Ben and Guy (see last page for boys).

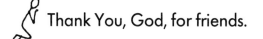 Thank You, God, for friends.

📖 Colossians 2:6

It was good at Boys' Brigade. They marched, played games, made models and had a Bible story and quiz. At the end, Captain reminded the boys that it was parade next Sunday. Guy wanted to know why they all went to church. Ben explained that church is where people who know and love Jesus like a friend meet, because they want to spend time with Him there.

Cut out, colour in. Bend tags to dress.

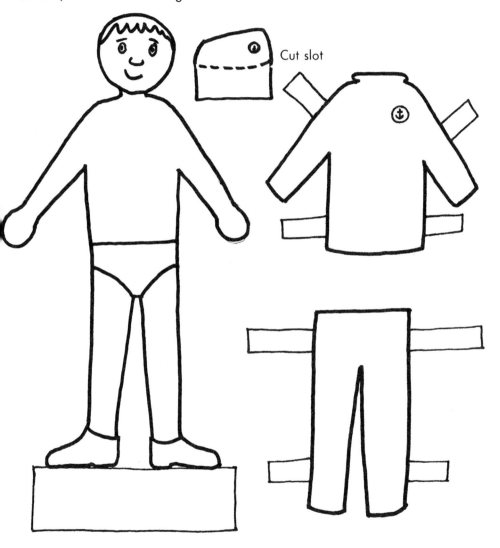

Cut slot

 Dear Jesus, I'm glad I can spend time with You.

While Ben was at school and Kate was at playgroup, Mum took Matthew to the toddler club at the church. He had a great time, crawling around while the older ones rode bikes and did 'cutting and sticking'. Mum met Mrs Patel, who had just moved into the area. She invited her and her husband to the church picnic.

Cut out shapes to make a jigsaw.

Thank You, God, for fun and picnics.

📖 Ephesians 4:6

Next Sunday the Ross family visited their grandparents and cousin Jo was there for the weekend, too. Jo goes to boarding school because her parents are missionaries in Africa. Gran and Grandpa live in a small village and their church is very old. The bells call everyone to church.

Help the Ross family get to church.

 Thank You, God, for different churches.

 Psalm 25:4-5

A cross was carried in front of the vicar and the choir as they walked into church. Behind them came the Guides and Scouts, parading just like in B.B. Before the children went out to Junior Church there was a christening. The children crowded around the font to watch. The parents and godparents promised to teach the baby, as he grew, about God and His love. Then the vicar sprinkled water on the baby's forehead.

Trace onto greaseproof or tracing paper and colour with felt tip pens to make stained glass window.

 Dear God, please help children like me to learn about You.

 Psalm 115:13

Ben and Kate then went out into the hall for Junior Church. After the sermon the vicar blessed the bread and wine, and the Junior Church came back in for communion. Everyone went up to kneel at the altar rail. The vicar gave the bread to the adults and blessed the children, while Grandpa, who was a lay preacher, followed behind with the wine.

Draw a picture of the building in which you worship.

Thank You, God, for your blessing.

Matthew 19:13–15

Some parents brought their children to Jesus for Him to pray for them. But the disciples tried to send them away. Jesus said, "Let the children come to me, because the Kingdom of Heaven belongs to such as these." Then He blessed them.

Colour in

Thank You, Jesus, that I can come to You.

📖 Galatians 6:10

After the service everyone stood chatting in the churchyard. Mum and Dad met lots of old friends and some people asked Jo about her Mum and Dad. Gran came out after putting fresh water in the flowers, and Grandpa arranged to go around and cut Mrs Gray's hedge. Then home for lunch!

Stick on scraps of coloured paper on to the flowers.

Thank You, God, for family and friends.

 Matthew 28:19

There was so much to talk about. Jo said that when she was with her Mum and Dad in Africa for the holidays, they had a baptismal service. Three new Christians were baptised in the river. They went right under the water and up again. It had been an exciting service and lots of people who didn't know Jesus came to watch.

Finger paint a riverside scene.

 Dear Jesus, please let everyone have a chance to know about You.

 Matthew 3:13–17

Jesus asked John to baptise Him in the river Jordan. But John said, "You ought to baptise me." Jesus replied, "God wants you to baptise me." So John did, and as Jesus was coming out of the water the Holy Spirit came down on Him in the form of a dove. A voice from Heaven said, "This is my own dear Son. I am very pleased with Him."

Colour in

 Dear God, help me to please You.

At home the family talked about Matthew's dedication plans. It would be good if all the family could be there. Maybe it could be when Auntie Kath and Uncle Jack were coming back from Africa on holiday. The Rosses' church had dedications instead of christenings. In this service they would say thank You to God for Matthew, and the church and family would promise to tell him about Jesus.

Colour in quilt, stick on cut straws or matchsticks for cot.

 Thank You, God, for new babies.

Luke 2:22–23; 27–28

Joseph and Mary took baby Jesus to the Temple in Jerusalem to dedicate Him to God. Simeon, who loved God, was there. The Holy Spirit had told him to go to the Temple. Simeon took Jesus in his arms and thanked God for Him.

Colour in

 Dear Jesus, help me to remember to say thank you.

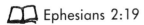 Ephesians 2:19

We are all part of God's family when we love Jesus, and so there are many friends in church who can help us learn more about Him.

Colour in

Thank You, God, that we can all be part of Your family.